MIKE FINK

A TALL TALE RETOLD AND ILLUSTRATED BY
STEVEN KELLOGG

MORROW JUNIOR BOOKS • NEW YORK

Colored inks, watercolors, and acrylics were used for the full-color artwork. The text type is 14-point Palatino.

1 2 3 4 5 6 7 8 9 10

CIP Data is available.

AUTHOR'S NOTE

Back in the days when America was a wild young country, the most daring and rugged frontiersmen were found aboard the Mississippi, Missouri, and Ohio river keelboats. They carried cargo thousands of miles from remote outposts down the vast network of waterways to New Orleans. Heading back upriver took superhuman strength because they had to pole the heavy boats against the current. Proud of their grit, the crewmen competed vigorously for the right to wear a red feather, which identified the strongest man on board. They loved to boast about the dangers they'd faced and the critters they'd licked; and they were convinced that a keelboatman could outdo anybody at anything. The most famous of all these ring-tailed roarers and river wrestlers was a fellow named Mike Fink.

To Arlen—another hero—with love

Mike was born not far from the Allegheny Mountains.
Right from the start, it was clear that he was destined for a
life of action. He hated being shut up indoors, and so
when he was only two days old he ran away from home.

There were rumors that Mike had joined a troupe of
acrobatic frogs that traveled from pond to pond.

Mike's grandfather came to fetch him. "The whole town's talking about a grandson of mine who's been hanging out with a gang of rowdy frogs!" he thundered. "From now on, you'll stay home and behave like a normal infant!"

Once again, Mike rebelled furiously against being confined indoors.

He leaped up and down on the bed with such force that he catapulted through the roof.

On the next leap, Mike rocketed high enough to see the vast network of rivers to the west. There he spotted the keelboats and heard the crews' hearty songs.

Mike plummeted back into the house, singing, "I'm going to be a keelboatman. Cock-a-doodle-doo!"

Once again, Mike set off a family uproar. "Keelboatmen are ruffians, rowdies, and riffraff," wailed his grandmother. "This new outrage will disgrace the family name forever!"

Mike's mother decided then and there that her son would be much happier if she raised him on the frontier, so the next morning they joined a wagon train heading west.

Mike loved the freedom of wilderness life. However, the sudden death of their ox threw his mother into despair. "How will we clear the land?" she cried. "How will we plow?" "Cheer up, Mamma," said Mike. "I can handle those chores." And he did.

HERE LIES
OWEN
Our Old OX.
I
think
he died
from
CHICKEN POX.
HE
WAS
OUR
FRIEND.

But Mike never stopped dreaming of becoming a keelboatman. He had heard that wrestling was their favorite sport, and it was also his. He was not tall for his age, but he was sturdy and quick. Even when he wrestled boys much bigger and older than himself, he usually came out on top.

Mike also showed an early talent for riflery. He called the family gun Bang All, and he soon became such a crackerjack marksman that he could shoot the shell off an egg.

Along about the time he turned sixteen, he entered a local shooting match. Each entrant had three chances to score.

Mike hit the bull's-eye on his first try, but his next two attempts left the target unmarked. "One lucky hit and two wild shots put you out of the running," chuckled the scorekeeper.

But Mike got the last laugh when he showed him all three bullets lined up behind the bull's-eye as neatly as peas in a pod.

Mike's skill with a rifle landed him a job as a scout, but he was still drawn westward by the memory of those great rivers.

Finally, Mike found himself face to face with Jack Carpenter, the King of the Keelboatmen. "Howdy," said Mike. "I'm looking for a job."

"This river cracks pip-squeaks like peanuts," said Carpenter. "Come back when you're ten feet taller, and then we'll find out if you're strong enough to pole your share of the load."

"I may be short," said Mike, "but I'm strong, and I'd like a chance to prove it."

"I'm stronger than a buffalo stampede and meaner than a rattlesnake with a bellyache!" snarled Carpenter. "If you can lick me, the job is yours—and so is this red feather."

"You've got yourself a deal!" cried Mike. "Cock-a-doodle-doo! Let's wrestle!"

Carpenter charged forward like a bull.

Then he hurled Mike hundreds of miles into the heart
of the Rocky Mountains.

"Well, that set me back a bit," admitted Mike, "but I'm determined to be a keelboatman." He decided to get in shape by wrestling with the grizzlies.

At first, those bears rolled him onto his back before he could say "Jack Carpenter."

But Mike kept trying, and little by little his strength increased until he was able to hold his own.

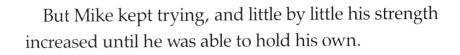

Finally, he decided to test himself by challenging Big Bart, the heavyweight champion of the Rockies.

When Mike came out on top, he knew he was ready for that keelboat job.

He sprinted across the Great Plains and found Jack Carpenter.

"Cock-a-doodle-doo! I'm back for round two! Let's wrestle!" hollered Mike.

Again, Carpenter charged like a bull, but this time Mike met him head-on.

They wrestled up and down the riverbanks for several weeks, kicking up tidal waves and toppling trees. Finally, Carpenter found himself locked helplessly in a Rocky Mountain grizzly-bear hug. "I'm licked," he gasped.

After the orneriness had been squeezed out of Jack
Carpenter, he became downright agreeable. With
Carpenter's help, Mike got the hang of navigating
so quickly that the crew voted to make him captain.

They sang and danced and celebrated all afternoon,
while the boat drifted lazily down the river toward
New Orleans.

Heading upriver was a different story. The boat had to be poled and pushed continually to prevent the powerful current from sweeping it backward. The men forged through rapids and up waterfalls, pausing occasionally to tangle with the man-eating alligators and enormous snapping turtles that lay in wait for them.

Whenever rival keelboats met, there were races on the water and games and sports on land. Men lined up by the dozens to try and win Mike's feather, but no one got the best of him. His hat began to look like a bonfire, and they called him the King of the Keelboatmen.

Mike loved all the rough-and-tumble excitement, but he also loved the times when the river was silent and still. He thought that his life as a keelboatman was just about perfect, and he hoped it would never end.

But then one morning, Mike saw dark clouds on the horizon. He was told that these were steamboats and that they were being sent to take over the river trade.

Mike hated the shriek of their whistles and the clatter of
their paddle wheels. He hated the foul-smelling smoke
that fogged the river as they churned past him.

Faster and larger steamboats kept arriving. They created traffic jams at the major ports that made it impossible for Mike and the other keelboat captains to unload their cargo.

THE ★ BUFFALO

MIGHTIEST BOAT AFLOAT

NATCHEZ
MISSISSIPPI

A showdown was sparked when a steamboat skippered by Hilton P. Blathersby shoved Mike's keelboat away from the dock. "This garbage scow is blocking river traffic and should be sunk!" hollered Blathersby.

"I'm King of the Keelboatmen!" roared Mike. "I'll fight for this dock! I'll fight for this river!"

"ALL HANDS PREPARE FOR NAVAL COMBAT!" bellowed Blathersby.

With whistles blowing, bells clanging, and smokestacks belching, the powerful steamboat charged forward like a rogue elephant.

For a moment, Mike managed to raise the prow of his monstrous opponent, forcing its stern under the water. But then its weight overwhelmed him, and Mike and his keelboat were gone.

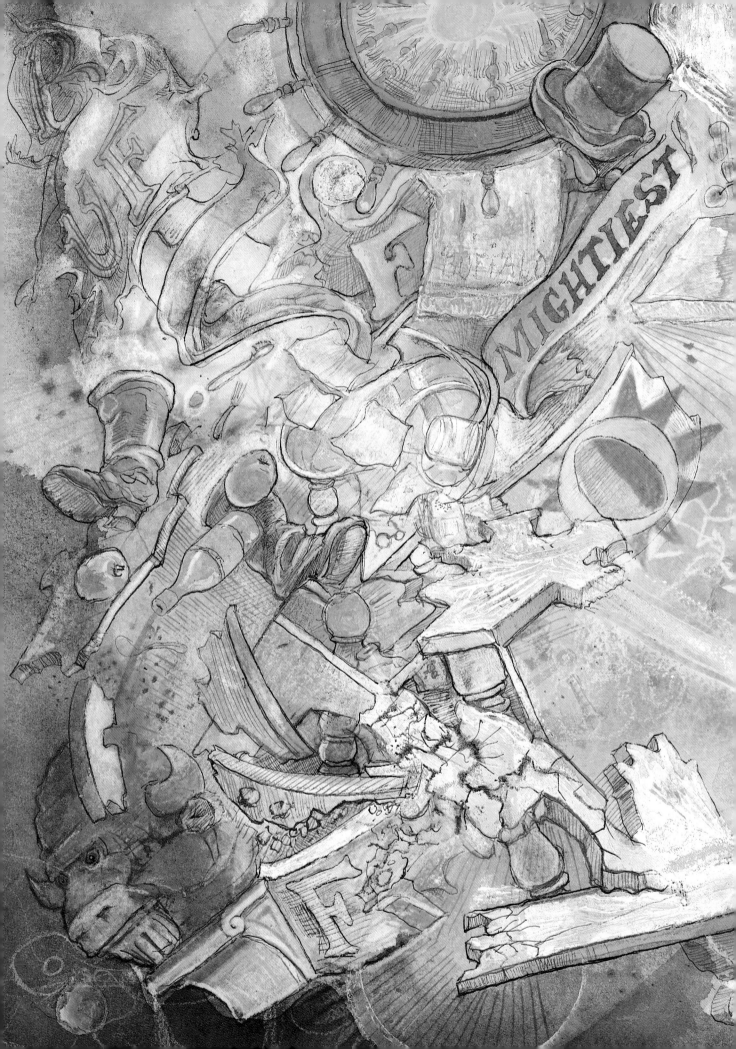

Blathersby was astonished to find Mike underneath his hat. "Cock-a-doodle-doo! I'm back for round two! Let's wrestle!" he cried.

Some say that Blathersby was thrown all the way to grizzly-bear country, but no one knows for sure.

As for Mike Fink, he's still cheered from one end of the river to the other as the undefeated King of the Keelboatmen.

He spotted Mike's hat from his lifeboat and ordered his men to row closer so he could collect the feathers. "After all," he said, "now *I'm* King of the Keelboatmen and King of the River."

One of the few survivors was Captain Blathersby.

A second later, the cold water that had rushed into the
steamboat's red-hot boilers set off an enormous explosion.